D0717413

THE RAKE'S PROGRESS
and
CHECKMATE

The Stories of the Ballets

by
MARION ROBERTSON

with decorations by
JOYCE MILLEN

LONDON
ADAM & CHARLES BLACK

First Published 1949
by A. & C. Black Ltd.,
4, 5 & 6 *Soho Square, London, W.*1

For list of books in the Series see page 96

MADE IN GREAT BRITAIN
PRINTED BY MORRISON AND GIBB LTD.
LONDON AND EDINBURGH

CONTENTS

PREFACE

THIS book tells the story of two ballets by Ninette de Valois, the most distinguished figure in the history of our national ballet. In the early days of the Sadler's Wells Company, Miss de Valois danced (she was formerly a dancer with Diaghilev), directed the Company, and created some of their finest ballets.

Since 1931, when the Company came into being with eight dancers, it has grown enormously. From this small beginning it has become a great Company with a reputation that extends far beyond this country. Its permanent home is now the Royal Opera House,

Covent Garden. The Company pays frequent visits to the Continent, and in October 1949 it paid its first visit to America. The advance bookings were said to be a record, even for the Metropolitan Opera House, New York. There is a Junior Company, the Sadler's Wells Theatre Ballet, and the Sadler's Wells School in Kensington, which provides a general education as well as training for ballet.

The person most responsible for this remarkable achievement is Ninette de Valois. But, while we applaud her magnificent work as Director, we must regret a little that she no longer has time to create new ballets for her Companies. We must, however, be grateful that two of her finest ballets—*The Rake's Progress* and *Checkmate*—have been retained in the current repertoire of the Sadler's Wells Ballet.

THE RAKE'S PROGRESS

INTRODUCTION

IT was in 1735 that Hogarth's famous series of moral pictures entitled " The Rake's Progress " first appeared. A somewhat similar series, " The Harlot's Progress " had been exhibited three years before, in 1732, and these two sets of " pictorialised moralisings," as they were called, proved highly successful. Hogarth was essentially a cynic in the same vein as Jonathan Swift and these comments on 18th-century life in

London are full of barbed jabs at con-
temporary society. Something of this
cynicism, too, has crept into the actual
moralising for, in spite of their sup-
posedly moral purpose in showing the
evils brought about by profligacy and
loose living, one cannot help seeing that
Hogarth was always in sympathy with
his fallen characters. The Rake's misfortunes, for instance, are implied rather
as being caused by bad luck and evil
companions than by his own behaviour
and we cannot help feeling that he
must have had some redeeming features
for The Betrayed Girl to have been so
constant in her love, which lasted even
to his last horrible days in Bedlam.

Hogarth's ultimate sincerity as a moral-
ist must remain open to enquiry, but his

mastery in telling a lively tale in pictures
cannot be denied, for each of these pictures is crammed with pungent comment
on the seamier side of 18th-century
London life and contains much interesting detail. It is fascinating, having seen
the ballet, to study again the pictures
and pick out the characters that have
been brought to life by Ninette de Valois
—the collection of rogues in the first
scene of the ballet ; the lively orgy scene
with the drunken women grouped round
the table, The Dancer rolling down her
stockings and The Rake in an advanced
state of inebriation (in the painting,
one of the women is seen to have just
stolen the Rake's watch and is handing
it to one of her companions) ; the gam-
bling scene, set in White's Club, a famous
London rendezvous of the time which

stood in St. James's; and the final scene in Bedlam, peopled by many of those pitiful figures that appear on the stage— The Gentleman with the Rope, the old violinist with his music tied across his empty head, the supposed King in his cell and the fashionable lady visitors on their sight-seeing trip. It is by comparing the ballet with the original pictures in this way that we can realise fully how faithfully and painstakingly Miss de Valois built up her ballet in order to keep it in period and create the authentic atmosphere of 18th-century London.

The original pictures comprise a series of eight which were reduced to six to give the ballet a more compact form; and the episode of The Rake's marriage to a wealthy woman, in the

hope that her money might serve to
settle his debts, was omitted in order to
leave the main story as simple and un-
complicated as possible since the in-
clusion of this marriage would obviously
have lengthened the ballet considerably
and probably have detracted from its
forcefulness in the process, for the whole
point of the story is enchanced by the
swift succession of events, each one
leading The Rake deeper and deeper into
trouble and debt and culminating in his
dreadful end.

The Scenario and Score

Miss de Valois' collaborators in this
work were Gavin Gordon and Rex
Whistler, the latter's first work for the
ballet. Gavin Gordon, to whom had
first occurred the notion of translating

Hogarth's pictures into a balletic idiom, is first and foremost a singer and studied both at the Royal College of Music in London and, subsequently, in Milan. He has been seen in London in many productions, including some of the famous Gaiety shows and, more recently, in the musical play *The Nightingale*. When he had completed both the scenario and the admirably descriptive score for *The Rake's Progress* he took them in the first place to Frederick Ashton, but the latter, feeling the subject to be outside his particular choreographic field of expression, suggested that they be shown to Ninette de Valois, whose particularly strong sense of period was already well known and who possessed the priceless gift of being able to create on the stage the

very breath and atmosphere of days long
past, and so it was that *The Rake's
Progress* came into being.

The Décor

The décor and costumes were designed
by Rex Whistler, a young artist whose
work for the legitimate theatre was
already well known, and they have
become as much an integral part of
the whole work as any part of the
music or the choreography. Who,
now, could conceive The Rake wearing
anything but his salmon-pink dressing
gown or his scarlet and gold coat; who
could picture The Dancer in any other
than bright, sunny yellow or The
Betrayed Girl in anything but her black
and red attire beneath her snowy
white apron and with her little white

cap set atop her hair? Some years later, Whistler designed the Sadler's Wells production of Fokine's *Spectre of the Rose,* and his exquisite set was the only one that I personally have ever really liked, for he followed the original conception of the story and turned the stage into as charming a bedroom as any young girl could desire, a room in which it was quite conceivable that a girl might fall into a reverie and dream of the spirit of the rose she had worn to a ball. In most of the modern presentations of the ballet, the poor girl is dumped into a bare and empty room, furnished with but a single chair (I often feel the designer grudges her even this and only includes it because the story calls for her to sit on something) which is no more conducive to romantic dreaming than is Liverpool Street station. Unhappily, Rex Whistler was killed on active service during the war and we can now only imagine the lovely work he might have done for the English ballet, had he lived. It is possible, too, that he might have done something highly original in the field of design for comic ballets as anyone will appreciate who has seen his wonderful little book of faces which may be turned either way up to reveal two faces in one and which are equally clever and amusing whichever way up they are seen.

Besides the two works already mentioned, he designed one other Wells Ballet—Ashton's lovely *The Wise Virgins* —and several plays including productions of *The Tempest*, *Victoria Regina*, *Love for*

Love, etc., but *The Rake's Progress* is the work by which he is most generally remembered in the ballet world and the only alteration that has been made to his original designs is the addition of a decorative frame which was created as a tribute to him by Oliver Messel, another distinguished British designer.

The Choreography

Of all Ninette de Valois' many ballets, *The Rake's Progress* is generally judged the finest and most universally successful (although, oddly enough, it was not nearly so popular when first produced) for it has been acclaimed not only in England, but in all the countries which the Sadler's Wells have visited during their European tours. It is in this work that her talent for creating vivid characters, her feeling for period and her keen observation have been used to their best advantage and blended together into something that has become one of the touchstones of English ballet. It was one of the first works to reveal that English ballet was no mere flash in the pan but a living force which was slowly but surely building itself up into a real art form and evolving for itself a peculiarly English idiom and it is, therefore, a ballet which will always have its own special niche in the Wells repertoire.

Apart from any historical significance, however, it will always retain its place because, above everything else, it is supremely entertaining. It has a good story to tell, its characters are vivid, lusty and excellently drawn and it holds our interest all the time. It is, too, a first-class ballet from the dancer's point of view for each rôle is a gem in itself and even the tiniest parts can be built up by individual touches into interesting cameos that all combine to add to the effect of the complete work.

To begin with, the part of The Rake himself is a veritable *tour de force* for any dancer for its dramatic scope is tremendous, ranging as it does from the pleasant conceits and frivolities of the first scene, by way of tipsy merrymaking, clashes with creditors and the hazards of the gaming table, to the eventual twitching horror of complete madness in Bedlam, with attempted murder at the last minute thrown in for good measure It is true that there are no complicated or technically difficult variations for the dancer to perform but, in their stead, the part calls for him to possess a mimetic range of uncommon strength and variety for he is the prop by which the whole ballet stands or falls.

The Rôles and their Creators

The original Rake, Walter Gore, never seemed to exploit fully the immense possibilities the rôle offered and it was not until Robert Helpmann took over that The Rake, as we know him to-day, really leapt to life and galvanised the whole work into brilliant, compelling action. How handsome and elegant he appears at first with his new clothes, his freshly curled wig, his petulant mouth and, the final touch of perfection, his black velvet patch set against the fashionable paleness of his complexion, and how infinitely more pathetic and horrible by contrast is the naked, contorted insanity that follows so hard on the heels of all this elegance.

The Betrayed Girl was first danced by
Alicia Markova, who was unhappily mis-
cast in the part. She had all the tenderness and pathos necessary but they were
of a spiritual, unearthly kind that were
out of place in this particular setting and
she lacked the underlying suggestion of
earthiness that is need to fit the Girl
into the general framework of the story
and make her a credible person. However, successors came along who were
more suited to the rôle and Elisabeth
Miller, Margot Fonteyn, Julia Farron
and, recently, Violetta Elvin, have all
scored signal successes in the part. It
was Elisabeth Miller who first succeeded
in showing the depths of feeling which
the young girl's love and devotion could
touch in us and she was followed by
Margot Fonteyn who was, perhaps, the

loveliest of any we have yet seen dance this part. Who will ever forget her tenderness, her quiet, unswerving devotion to her erring lover or the way in which she wrung our hearts with pity as she danced in the nightmare prison to an accompanying air piped on a melancholy flute ?

There are two other outstanding rôles in the ballet, both dancing ones as opposed to the mainly mimed rôle of The Rake—The Dancing Master and The Gentleman with the Rope—and these were created by Harold Turner who danced them both on the opening night and fairly stole the limelight from the principals in so doing. Two more widely contrasted characters could not well be conceived than the elegantly

capering figure in blue of the first scene
and the twisted, grovelling creature in
his tattered old brown jacket of the last,
but Turner, always one of the virtuosos
of English male dancing, was equally at
home as either and well deserved his
success. This success in both the parts,
incidentally, has only been rivalled by
one other dancer—Gordon Hamilton—
who is, in most ways, a complete anti-
thesis of Turner but possesses something
of his virtuosity though it is translated
in a completely different manner.

Hamilton's Dancing Master, for instance, is so spruce and well-groomed
that we can never imagine him ever
going to bed, never picture him remov-
ing his carefully arranged wig, his
dandified blue satin coat and breeches

or his completely wrinkle-free white stockings—we feel quite sure he sits up all night for fear of disarranging his *toilette* since it could surely never be accomplished quite so perfectly again. Turner, on the other hand, was a little more human and credible and this applied also to his pitiful madman of the final scene, for Hamilton's lunatic is a tiny, wizened creature that it is hard to believe could ever have been a sane human being. Yet I have to confess that, for me at least, there is a particular fascination in both Hamilton's interpretations for their very unreality seems somehow to fit more easily, more inevitably, into the unreal, larger-than-life world of ballet where anything can happen and generally does—sooner or later !

THE RAKE'S PROGRESS

A Ballet in Six Scenes.

Book and Music by Gavin Gordon.

Scenery and Costumes by Rex Whistler.

Choreography by Ninette de Valois.

First produced at the Sadler's Wells Theatre, May 20th, 1935.

THE RAKE'S PROGRESS

A Ballet in Six Scenes.

Book and Music by Gavin Gordon.

Scenery and Costumes by Rex Whistler.

Choreography by Ninette de Valois.

First produced at the Sadler's Wells Theatre, May 20th, 1935.

Cast at the first performance

The Rake	Walter Gore
The Betrayed Girl ..	Alicia Markova
Her Mother	Ailne Phillips
The Rake's Friend	William Chappell
The Dancer	Ursula Moreton
The Dancing Master	Harold Turner
The Gentleman with the Rope	
	Harold Turner
The Tailor ..	Claude Newman
The Jockey	Richard Ellis
The Fencing Master	John Byron
The Bravo	Maurice Brooke
The Hornblower ..	Frank Staff
The Ballad Singer ..	Joy Newton

Ladies of the Town, Creditors, Gamblers, Lunatics, Visitors, etc.

The overture begins stridently as the curtain rises to reveal a dropcloth depicting a street lined on either side by solid Georgian houses and with a statue in the centre The period atmosphere is immediately captured for us and we are back in the 18th-century in a street in the region of Covent Garden. We find ourselves first in the interior of one of the great houses where The Rake is holding his morning levee. The set is a simple one to allow for easy changing —three walls with a door in both the

left- and right-hand walls and with
windows at the back. In the centre of
the room stands The Rake and grouped
about him are some of the tradesmen
and doubtful beings that always spring
up like mushrooms around someone
become newly rich; there is a jockey,
a bravo (a ruffian who, if paid sufficiently
well, undertakes to remove conveniently
any person or persons he is told) a horn
player, a fencing master, a dancing
master seated at a table with an expression of supercilious boredom on his
delicate features and an old, bent tailor
who is busy with tape measure and pins
fitting The Rake for his splendid new
scarlet coat.

In turn the others come forward to
extort money from the rich young man

—The Jockey describes the excitement of riding and jumping on horseback and tells of a recent success he has had and The Fencing Master displays the elegance and skill of his art, whilst The Bravo walks The Rake up and down whispering to him all the time and offering his services whenever they may be required. Now The Hornblower steps forward and plays a tune—The Rake is enchanted and nothing will do but he must try and play himself—not very successfully he finds.

Now at last the new coat is finished. The Rake is relieved of his salmon-coloured dressing gown and black cap and stands in scarlet breeches and white silk shirt with billowing sleeves. Carefully he adjusts his curled wig tied back

with a black bow, dons the new coat
and stands back for his new-found
friends to express their sycophantic
admiration. Now, all having received
bags of money from him, they leave and
The Rake is left alone with The Dancing
Master who picks up his tiny violin
(known as a " kit ") and commences the
lesson. His wealthy client, however, is
very clumsy indeed and cannot follow
the quick, neat movements of the elegant
figure in its short, flared, blue satin coat,
blue breeches, white stockings and shiny
black dancing pumps. Time after time
the young man tries a step and each
time trips over his own feet, becoming
more exasperated on every occasion
until The Dancing Master finally loses all
patience with him and, casting away his
kit, sits down in a huff. Now there is an

interruption as The Betrayed Girl enters.
She takes tiny steps on *pointe* and is like
a leaf driven before a strong wind, for
close on her heels comes her old harridan
of a mother who pushes her reluctant
daughter before her.   The Girl wears a
black skirt with a red bodice, a white
apron and a white cap on her head and
we can see at once that she is a sweet,
simple creature who, on some past
occasion, has fallen victim to the charms
and blandishments of The Rake.   The
Rake's look of discomfort when he sees
her bears this out and the Mother runs to
him, demanding some reparation for her
daughter's betrayal.   The young man
manages to appease her wrath with a
gift of money and she then takes herself
off again, still pushing her poor daughter
who is crying bitterly.

The Dancing Master, who has been surveying the scene with the liveliest curiosity, enquires as to the identity of the Girl and, when The Rake confides his indiscretion, looks suitably shocked but we cannot help feeling that he could tell much livelier tales himself, nor do we doubt that the story will be all over the town within the next day or two. Now the dancing lesson is resumed ; at last The Rake manages to execute a step without tripping up and, leaving him to congratulate himself, the drop curtain falls with The Dancing Master capering daintily before it, expressing by his capers both personal satisfaction in his own practised lightness and agility, and contempt for his rich patron who, for all his money, is yet clumsy and awkward As he dances, passers-by come and go—

three ladies of the town hiding their
faces behind black fans over which they
cast flirtatious looks at the elegant, blue-
clad figure; The Betrayed Girl, still
being subjected to her mother's re-
proaches, and a small serving maid,
wearing a blue dress and white cap and
apron and clutching to her breast a fat
bottle of wine as she runs as fast as
she can to some unknown destination.

When the drop curtain rises again, it
is on a room in one of the more dis-
reputable houses of the district. Again
the set is simple, but this time there is a
very tumbled bed in the background
which immediately and economically
gives a clue to the nature of the house—
should the audience be in any doubt.
A few of the ladies are chattering and

laughing together in the foreground as
the serving maid whom we saw in the
street enters with the bottle of wine she
had been sent out to purchase. There is
a prevalent air of general excitement.
Evidently company is expected and
here comes the Rake's friend, richly
dressed in black velvet and silver. The
women fall on him with glee and they
dance wildly about the room until the
door is thrown roughly open and in
staggers The Rake, already quite drunk
and ready for an uproarious evening's
entertainment. He is loudly and osten-
tatiously welcomed. His favourite, The
Dancer, greets him. She wears a yellow
dress, bright red stockings and carries a
large, round tray, which she places
on the floor. Sitting down, she lifts up
her skirt and, slowly and provocatively,

rolls down her scarlet stockings to her ankles, much to the glee of The Rake and his friend, and then dances on the tray she has set down, showing plenty of red stocking and bare leg in the process. The Rake is delighted and, leering to himself, bends down to obtain a better view.

Now the orgy really gets going—they drink and laugh, quarrel and are pacified, drink again and then there enters a small troup of itinerant musicians to add to the fun. Their Ballad Singer carols a popular air and, after some difficulty, The Rake staggers across the room and joins in with her, the effect being rather spoilt by his tendency to hiccup in the middle of a note. However, nobody seems to mind and they all join in at the tops of their shrill voices, while one of the women provides an imaginary accompaniment with her stays which she has removed and is playing as an accordion. The scene gets wilder and wilder; now they are all hopelessly and gloriously drunk and The Dancer has taken her stockings right off and is running about waving them in the air, closely pursued by The Rake who has set his heart on getting them from her. At last he succeeds and, climbing up on to the table, he stands there rocking and lurching, throwing the stockings and handfuls of coins across the room while the dishevelled women dance about him and grovel on the floor after the gold until finally they all collapse in a happy, befuddled heap.

Quite exhausted after this carouse, we find ourselves once again in the street where three of The Rake's creditors are assembling and preparing to present accounts. The Betrayed Girl passes on an errand and, recognising the men, looks at the bills and discovers their intention. Along comes The Rake, arrogant and self-assured as ever, but his expression quickly changes to dismay on seeing his creditors come to dun him. The Girl, unable to bear the sight of the man she loves in such a plight (although brought on entirely by himself), brings out the little bag containing all her savings and offers it in settlement of the debts. The tradesmen accept it and depart, satisfied for the time being at least, and The Girl is left alone, looking wistfully up at the grand façade of the Rake's

house which is as cold and indifferent to her as its occupant, for he has given her only the most perfunctory thanks for her generosity.

The next scene takes us to White's Club where some highly suspicious-looking gamblers are waiting for The Rake to join them in a game; already the cards and dice-box stand ready in the centre of a baize-covered table on which shines the only bright light in the room, the remainder being shrouded in semi-darkness. As The Rake enters, we see that now his fine clothes are torn and soiled and he has lost his magnificent scarlet coat. The game begins, but with every deal of the cards or throw of the dice luck is against him. As we look at his fellow-players, we doubt if it can only be bad luck and suspect that a fair amount of cheating, using of loaded dice and " dealing from the bottom " is going on. Now the final throw is made and, seeing his last coin lost and ruin staring him in the face, The Rake snatches off his wig and casts himself to the ground and, by the suddenly vacant expression of his face and the horrible staring of his eyes, we know that we are looking on madness. The curtain mercifully falls on the dreadful scene and, once more, we are in the street.

The Betrayed Girl is waiting outside the Fleet debtors' prison to learn her lover's fate and, as she waits, she works continuously at the embroidery by which she earns her living. Her dance is slow and wistful and her little feet beating on

the pavement echo the sad beating of
her heart.

For the last time the curtain rises,
this time on the bare, stone interior of a
madhouse. Four of the pitiful inmates
sit about, staring vacantly into their own
distorted worlds and in two barred cells
at the back are a further two, one who
fancies he is a king, the other believing
himself to be the Pope. One of the
men in the foreground holds a piece of
rope and as he shuffles to his feet and
begins to dance with it, it seems to take
on an obscene life of its own—first it is
a writhing snake, now a lash, now a
gallows noose ready to be placed about
a man's neck, now again it takes the
form of a slippery monster. Just as the
horror becomes almost too intense, the

door flies open and The Rake is pushed through on to the floor. He wears only his red breeches and his ravaged body twitches and strains as he rushes to the door and attempts vainly to open it, scratching and clawing at it in a frenzy until he finally falls to the ground in despair.

In turn, the other inmates of the cell come forward, each wrapped in his own particular shroud of madness ; one fancies he is a card player, another carries a telescope through which he peers, sighting invisible fleets seen many long years before, and a third is wrapped in a sheet and capers about, playing all the while on an old violin and pausing now and then to read his music which he wears tied to his head. They are a pitiful enough brotherhood, bound together by mutual ties of madness, but the worst sight of all is The Rake who still lies on the floor, twitching and staring blankly into space.

All at once The Betrayed Girl arrives and, though appalled by the dreadful condition of her lover, she runs to him for it is not in her simple, steadfast heart to desert a loved one in his distress. But he does not recognise her and while she tries to soothe and comfort him, tries to bring a spark of recognition into the vacant eyes, three fashionable ladies come sightseeing and stare curiously at the wrecks of humanity in the cell. There is something peculiarly horrible in their ghoulish curiosity and the lunatics huddle together and try to hide

themselves, aware for a brief moment of the pathetic sight they must present. As these sensation-seekers leave, The Rake is galvanised into a final burst of demoniac energy. His body contorts in agony and, in a sudden murderous fit, he tries to strangle The Girl but is seized by a last paroxysm and falls back dead at the feet of the one who, through all his misfortunes, has never ceased to love him.

CHECKMATE

CHECKMATE

INTRODUCTION

THE recent revival of Ninette de Valois'
ballet *Checkmate* at Covent Garden
has brought this work back into the
repertoire of the Sadler's Wells company after a lapse of something like
seven years, for this was one of the
works that had to be abandoned after
the scenery and costumes were lost
during the Company's flight from Holland
during the invasion in May, 1940. The
other works that suffered in a like
manner, such as *The Rake's Progress*

and *Façade* were revived during the subsequent war years but no attempt was made to revive *Checkmate* until 1947. Now that it has come, however, the revival has proved well worth while and appears to great advantage on the vast Covent Garden stage. E. McKnight Kauffer reconstructed almost exactly his original costumes, set and dropcloth which appear as attractive to-day as on their first appearance in 1937. Mr. McKnight Kauffer is better known as a poster artist than as a theatrical designer (his posters for the London Passenger Transport Board, for instance, are familiar everywhere) but his designs for *Checkmate* indicate that the very qualities that distinguish his posters—bright, clear colours and broad, bold lines—are ideal for the ballet, too.

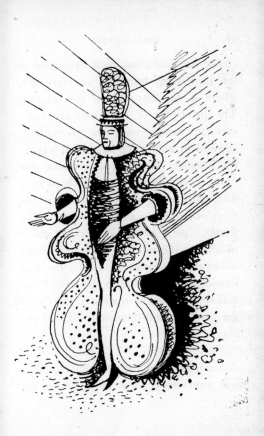

The game of chess itself originated in the East many hundreds of years ago, where it was first known as chequers. The principles of the game are fairly easy to master once the movements allowed to each piece have been learnt ; for instance, the King and Queen can move in any direction, the Bishops only diagonally, etc., while the Queen is the most powerful piece on the board. The Rooks, or Castles, can only move parallel to the sides of the board, either backwards or forwards, and in the Red Castle's first entrance in the ballet, this rule is suggested by their stiff, jerky progressions up and down the sides of the stage.

According to C. W. Beaumont, chess was previously used as a theme for

ballet as long ago as 1607 when a
Ballet des Echecs was performed in
Paris. Whether or not that ballet pur-
ported to move the pieces about in the
same way as they moved in an actual
game of chess we do not know, but de
Valois and Arthur Bliss (who wrote the
book for *Checkmate*) made no such
attempt, preferring to give individual
characteristics to a few of the main
pieces and then weave about them a
story of the eternal struggle between
Love and Death, or good and evil,
whichever way one cares to look at it.
The pieces thus selected and brought
to life have curiously potent personali-
ties and their very animation has about
it something of the sinister quality that
I always find in the court cards of a pack
of ordinary playing cards. Somehow

or other, those Kings and Queens of Diamonds, Spades, etc., always strike me as being evil and sly and I never even trust the chubby geniality of the Hearts, who are so unbelievably bland that I cannot help wondering what goes on behind their unchanging smiles.

In the same way, the pieces in *Checkmate* have something of this slyness and one wonders, as in the case of the court cards, how they spend their days and nights when they are left to their own devices; how they rule their subjects and manage their kingdoms. Idle speculation, perhaps, but curiously fascinating. Incidentally, this is one of the very few ballets in which the eventual outcome results in the overthrowing of good and the triumph of evil, for generally, good manages to re-assert itself just in time for the final curtain. Another ballet in which this occurs is *Miracle in the Gorbals* (physically, at any rate), while *Dante Sonata* does not attempt to decide but leaves the two factions still involved in their endless battle for supremacy.

The Choreographer

As a choreographer, Ninette de Valois has always had one fault which tended to spoil some of her finest work—a too great attention to detail which, at its worst, has been carried to excess to produce a fussy, over-laden effect. *The Prospect Before Us* is one of the most obvious examples of this, for there is so much going on at the same time that it is impossible to see everything and, while watching some amusing piece of

by-play, a development of the main story
is very easily lost. Unfortunately, this
ballet has the additional drawback of
being divided up into several scenes, a
device which is always difficult to carry
off successfully as an audience tends to
lose interest when the action of the
ballet it is watching is continually being
held up to allow for changes of scenery,
etc. It therefore says much for de
Valois' choreography (and Robert Helpmann's unforgettable piece of clown-
ing as Mr. O'Reilly—one of his most
brilliant parts) that the ballet is as good
as it is, in spite of these obvious
weaknesses.

Amongst her other works, *The Gods
go a-Begging* is a charming pastoral and
Promenade a character etching that was

gay and amusing when the leading rôle
was danced by Gordon Hamilton, for
whom it was created, but which lost
most of its point when the part was
taken by anyone else, for no other
dancer has ever come anywhere near
equalling Hamilton's agile, finicky little
cameo. One work which, however,
always retains a particular atmosphere
and effect of its own is *The Haunted
Ballroom*. The telling of this type of
story has been attempted many times
and in varying forms but no one,
perhaps, has succeeded as well as de
Valois, who has imparted just the air of
mystery and impending tragedy for
which the story calls. She has been
considerably helped by Motley's imagi-
native décor and costumes, particularly
by the wispy, grey garments of the

apparitions in the second scene, since the trailing sleeves add ghostliness to the simplest of choreography and produce the requisite effect. Who, too, will ever forget Alicia's superb red velvet gown and her wonderful fan which is used so expressively that it almost seems to speak. These last-mentioned three ballets are now danced by the Wells Theatre Ballet where they have been most valuable additions to the repertoire which is gradually being built up by this young and lively company.

Checkmate has come off lightly on the charge of fussiness but has fallen down on another count—one or two of the variations go on far too long and end up by losing their dramatic force through sheer overstatement. The most

c

outstanding example of this is the struggle between the Black Queen and the Red Knight which would be so much more effective were it only a little shorter and contained less repetition. This *pas de deux* is the virtual highlight of the whole story and a little judicious pruning would make the world of difference to its ultimate power. Apart from this, the general pattern moves along strong, broad lines with each of the principal characters furnished with just the right choreography to best bring out his or her characteristics and thus clarify the story.

There are some slight differences between the present revival and the original ballet. In the original version, for instance, only Death appeared on

the stage after the slaying of the Red
Knight and led out the funeral procession, but now both Death and Love
appear, the latter sorrowful and down-
cast at the relentless vanquishing of the
side he champions. On her first entry,
the Black Queen used to wear a red
rose and not, as now, a black one ; the
exit of the Red Queen has been slightly
altered and so, too, has the *pas de deux*
of the Red Knight and the Black Queen,
while the ending has been changed so
that now the Black Queen snatches off
the old King's crown whereas, before,
he removed it himself before he met his
death. However, these small differences
detract nothing from the power and
excitement of the ballet as a whole and
it still remains a most gripping piece of
stagecraft.

The Rôles and their Creators

The part of the first Red Knight was
danced on the first night of the revival,
November 18th, 1947, by Harold
Turner, whose performance must have
brought back memories to many people,
for he was the creator of the rôle and
danced it when the ballet was first produced. It is a perfect " Turner rôle "
and gives full play to his technique

which is still remarkable, particularly in the Sadler's Wells Company where, as a general rule, insufficient attention is still paid to male technique, the emphasis being laid on acting and miming. The part is now also being danced by Michael Somes, whose elegant style fits well into the character of the chivalrous, romantic warrior.

The Black Queen was originally danced by June Brae, and anyone who did not see her in the part can well imagine how exciting her performance must have been by recalling her in *Adam Zero,* in which she had a part of similar dramatic scope and intensity. Technically, she may sometimes have been disappointing and erratic but her miming was always strong and telling and her wonderful smile could be, in turn, evil, seductive or gloating. The rôle is now shared by Pamela May (The first Red Queen), Violetta Elvin and Beryl Grey and it is, perhaps, the last who is the most successful, for the seductive quality of her dancing (not really seen in this light since she appeared as Duessa in *The Quest*) and her lovely, broad, generous movements convey all the requisite queenliness, allure and cunning that alternate throughout the part, masking the Black Queen's underlying cruelty by her outward beauty.

The Red King, of course, was one of Robert Helpmann's many memorable parts and his interpretation of the feeble, tottering old man suggested

all his present weakness whilst yet
hinting at the past glories and bravery
of his youth. It may be of interest
to mention that when *Checkmate*
received its first performance in Paris,
Helpmann, having injured one of his legs,
had been unable to rehearse properly
beforehand so that it was not until he
was actually on the stage on that first
night that the rest of the cast really knew
how the part was to be interpreted.
The Red Queen was danced by Pamela
May, and it was this rôle which gave
her the first real opportunity of revealing
herself as something more than a lovely
and competent dancer, for her sensitive
miming and her tender solicitude for
her weak, aged husband made of the
comparatively small part something
worthy to stand beside Helpmann's own

performance—no small praise for any dancer.

So after a lapse of many years, one more ballet has been revived to add yet another native work to the Sadler's Wells repertory and to help repair the losses of 1940.

CHECKMATE

A ballet in One Scene with a Prologue

Book and Music by Arthur Bliss

Scenery and Costumes by
E. McKnight Kauffer

Choreography by Ninette de Valois

First produced at the
Théâtre des Champs-Élysées, Paris
June, 1937

First performance in London at the
Sadler's Wells Theatre,
October 5th, 1937

Cast at the first performance

Two Chess Players	{ Frederick Ashton Alan Carter
First Red Knight	Harold Turner
Second Red Knight	William Chappell
Black Queen	June Brae
Red King	Robert Helpmann
Red Queen	Pamela May
Black Knights	{ Richard Ellis Michael Somes
Red Castles	{ Leslie Edwards John Nicholson
Black Castles	{ Joy Newton Anne Spicer
Red Bishops	{ Claude Newman Paul Regloff
Red Pawns	{ Molly Brown, Joyce Farron, Jill Gregory, Wenda Horsbrugh, Elisabeth Kennedy, Joan Leaman, Laurel Martyn, Linda Sheridan.
Black Pawns	{ Margot Fonteyn, Mary Honer, Pamela May, Elizabeth Miller.

As the curtain rises, Love and Death are seen seated on either side of a small table on which stands a chessboard with the red and black pieces all set out for the commencement of the game. Behind them is a dropcloth of bluish-grey across which there extends a giant hand from which radiate lines in all directions as if to signify the far-reaching powers of the hand, or its owner, and the effect is eerily to suggest the Fate that watches over and directs the grim tragedy about to be played out on the chessboard. Death is dressed in grey and red; on his head is a helmet and a heavy cloak falls

from his shoulders : Love is dressed in
blue, also with a long cloak about his
shoulders and a helmet which he removes
to reveal his strong, youthful features
and his head of shining golden hair that
gleams like a halo. For a while they
study the pieces in silence, then Death
slowly reaches out a bony hand and
moves one of the Black pieces he champions. The two figures rise to their
feet and move the board slowly round
on the table until their respective pieces
are once more before them. Love
studies the board but cannot reply to
Death's move—he is checkmated, and
the two warriors playing their ghostly
game are veiled in darkness.

The setting changes to the scene of
the battle—a huge chessboard spread

out before a backcloth of multi-hued
cubist design in red, green, orange, black,
yellow and other colours, on which
again appear the radiating lines of the
first dropcloth. Against this back wall
is the Red King's throne raised up on a
small dias and before it are set the Red
Pawns, perky little pieces who dance
briskly backwards and forwards, step-
ping in and out of the black and white
squares of the board. The two Red
Knights enter, brave, chivalrous fighters
who look tall and elegant in their red
costumes picked out in orange and gold
and with ribbons flying from their
sleeves and helmets. Closely in their
wake come the two Black Knights
whose black and silver attire gives them a
sinister aspect and who are more ruthless
warriors than their red counterparts.

Their appearance heralds the arrival of their Queen who is the most powerful of all the pieces. She is strikingly beautiful in her black, grey and silver costume and she steps proudly and arrogantly across the board, contemptuously regarding the Red pieces who are assembling against her. Yet, to gain her own ends, she can turn her arrogance into a seductive, enticing charm and when she sees that the Red Knights are not afraid of her or of her warriors, she changes her tactics and tries to allure them in order that they may betray their King and Queen and deliver victory into her own hands. One of the Knights refuses to be influenced by her blandishments and turns his back on her, but the other is more romantically inclined and finds the Black Queen's charms too

strong for him to resist. Dazzled by
her beauty, he watches as she is carried
round by her two Knights, then tries to
approach her, ignoring his companion,
the second Red Knight, who tries to
bar his path and warn him that he is
falling in love with his bitterest enemy.
Before she leaves, and enchanted with
the success of her wiles, the Queen
throws down a black rose which the
infatuated Red Knight retrieves. All
the pieces then leave the board and,
left alone, the Knight dances a dashing
mazurka expressing his love and his
foolish joy as he believes that his love is
returned by the beautiful Black Queen.

The Red Pawns return bearing the
Red standard before which the two
Knights kneel to receive the blessing of

the Bishops prior to the battle which is soon to begin, and when the ceremony is completed the two Red Castles arrive. These are tall and terrifying creatures who move stiffly and menacingly and create a horrid impression as of robots in their long, straight coats and grotesque head-dresses which completely mask their faces. They are inhuman beings who will seek to crush the enemy by brute force, having no time for the battle etiquette observed by the Knights. Now, their subjects having all assembled, the King and Queen arrive. She is fair and gentle and tenderly helps along her husband who is excessively weak and helpless. So feeble is he, indeed, that it is with the greatest difficulty that he is able to cross the board to reach his throne and, were it not for the supporting arms of his Queen, he would certainly fall to the ground before he reaches it. However, at last he is safely enthroned with his Queen at his left side, the two Knights on either side of him, flanked by the Bishops, and the remainder of the pieces arranged in their appointed places. They are ready for the attack.

With their Queen at their head brandishing her sword, the Black pieces enter and the battle begins. The two opposing pairs of Knights face each other and appraise each other's strength, while the Black Queen darts in and out of the fray and amuses herself by making vicious advances at the Red King who cowers on his throne, terrified by her onslaught and not daring to think of the outcome should she be victorious

As she kneels triumphantly before him with her Black pieces ranged formidably about her, the Red King orders his Bishops to move forward but the Queen scornfully sweeps them back and runs past them to the foot of the throne, indicating that they are no barrier to her progress.

Seeing her husband's terror at this setback, the Red Queen steps forward and tries to woo the unrelenting Black Queen with sweet words and pleas but her prayers are all to no avail and the Black Queen, smiling mockingly to herself, finally gives her to the two Black Knights who carry their prize off in triumph, heedless of her cries for help.

Horrified by this heartless move, the

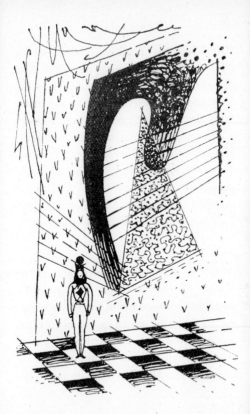

Red King has now no choice but to advance his champion, the first Red Knight, who resolutely thrusts aside his love and prepares to battle to the death with the enemy Queen. There follows a terrific struggle as the two strongest pieces on the board meet in open combat. Now the Knight seems to be the more successful, now the Queen, and as he watches them, the old King's spirits fluctuate with the success or otherwise of his Knight.

At last the Queen is overcome and is forced to retreat before her superior opponent who compels her to drop her sword and sink down on to her knees, while behind them the Red King smiles with heartfelt relief at the subjugation of the enemy. The Red Knight raises his sword to kill the Queen but, as he is about to lower his arms to strike the death blow, she has a desperate flash of inspiration. Slowly she tilts her head back so that she is looking up at her conqueror and her arms creep upwards in a voluptuous caress as she smiles seductively at him. In that moment she gains her victory, for her smile has turned the fearless fighter once more into the man who is in love with her and his arms fall helplessly to his sides. Cunningly she takes the sword from his hand and he makes no move to resist for he knows now that he cannot kill the woman he loves. Turning away, he retires across the board, unable to face either her or his King and the latter is once more filled with horror at seeing certain victory so foolhardily and inexplicably flung away. But as the Knight stands reproaching himself, behind him the Black Queen has stealthily picked up both his sword and her own and, caring nothing for his love or his bravery, creeps up behind him and viciously stabs him in the back. Stunned and uncomprehending, he turns to face her as if seeking an explanation of her treachery, but even as he staggers towards her, his strength fails and he falls dead before the throne. From either side enter Love and Death who regard the lifeless body while Death drops his glove upon it as a mark of his triumph. Saddened by this loss of his gallant subject, Love slowly retires, leaving Death in proud possession of the board in company with his victorious subject, the Black Queen. Slowly and

sadly the Red pieces gather up their
fallen hero and, with one Bishop leading
them and the other bringing up the rear,
they form a funeral procession and carry
him away.

Death also retires and now the Red
King is left alone and undefended,
shrinking back on his throne and trem-
bling with fear at the fate he knows can
no longer be averted for very long.
Bathed in a brilliant white light,
the Black Queen dances before him,
flourishing the two swords and flaunting
her victory in his face. Backwards and
forwards across the board she moves,
now in the white squares, now in the
black, but always moving nearer and
nearer to the throne and its solitary
miserable occupant who watches every

sinuous movement as though hypno-
tised. At last she stands before him
and he anticipates immediate death, but
regarding him haughtily she deems him
a foe unworthy of her steel and will not
touch him herself. Proudly she turns
away from him and goes to rally her
warriors for the final skirmish.

Left alone on the board, the old man
gathers the last shreds and tatters of his
failing strength together in a bid to
escape but as he totters across the great
chequered floor, going in turn to each
corner of the board, his way is blocked
every time by the menacing Black pieces,
Knights, Castles and Pawns, who are
carrying long poles with which they drive
him backwards towards the throne, now
a mere mocking symbol of his former

power, and cut off his chances of escape.
His strength is all but exhausted and he

gasps for breath but he has not yet given up all hope of getting away.

All the pieces dance mockingly round him but he successfully breaks through their ranks, only to find the two terrible Black Castles blocking his path. Driven by them to retreat, he sinks back on to a platform made by the criss-crossed staves and is carried triumphantly round and back to the throne from whence he started. (This whole sequence, indeed, is very like one of those terrible nightmares in which one is trying desperately to escape from someone or something, only to keep returning to the place that one started out from and consequently making no headway at all.) Again he tries to escape but the Pawns have lined up in couples so that their staves bar his path. Now the Black Queen enters for the kill, smiling tauntingly as she regards her feeble prey, worn out with his fruitless attempts to evade the death she has decreed. She is lifted on high by her Knights and as she raises her sword, the old man suddenly remembers his past glories and the fact that, above everything, he is a King and must face his death in a fitting manner. With his last ounce of strength he draws himself up to his full height and bravely turns to the Queen that he may meet his death as befits a King, rather than be stabbed in the back. The Queen, unimpressed by this last gallant gesture, stabs him and he falls dead, but not before the Queen has snatched off his crown and thus sealed her final triumph.

THE BALLET POCKET SERIES

† *Two ballets in one volume.*